On The Job
at School

by Jessica Cohn

RED
CHAIR
·PRESS·

Please visit our website at **www.redchairpress.com** for more high-quality products for young readers.

Publisher's Cataloging-In-Publication Data

Cohn, Jessica.
 On the job at school / by Jessica Cohn.

 pages : illustrations ; cm. -- (On the job)

 Summary: "You may think you know who keeps your school running. You know teachers and coaches, but there are many important careers in education. Let's do our homework by going On the Job at School."--Provided by publisher.

 Includes writing activity and first-person interview.
 Includes bibliographical references and index.
 ISBN: 978-1-63440-108-1 (library hardcover)
 ISBN: 978-1-63440-114-2 (paperback)
 ISBN: 978-1-937529-52-9 (ebook)

 1. Education--Vocational guidance--Juvenile literature. 2. Schools--Juvenile literature. 3. Education--Vocational guidance. 4. Schools. I. Title. II. Title: At school

LB1775 .C64 2016
371.0023   2015953629

Illustration credits: p. 4, 7, 8, 9, 12, 13, 14, 15, 19, 20, 25, 27, 28, 30, 32: Lauren Scheuer

Photo credits: Cover, p. 6-7, 7, 10-11, 18-19, 25: iStock; p. 1, 3, 4-5, 5 (middle), 8, 9, 14 (bottom), 19, 22 (left), 23 (left), 24 (top): Dreamstime; p. 5 (top), 12-13, 13, 14 (top), 15, 20, 21 (top, bottom), 22 (right), 23 (right), 24 (middle), 26 (top, bottom, bottom right), 27 (top, middle), 28, 29: Shutterstock; p. 5 (bottom): Catalogue of the Boston Public Latin School; p. 16: Life Touch; p. 17: Diana Parker; p. 32: Nathan Cohn

This series first published by:
Red Chair Press LLC   PO Box 333   South Egremont, MA 01258-0333

Printed in the United States of America

Distributed in the U.S. by Lerner Publisher Services. www.lernerbooks.com

0516 1 WRZF16

Table of Contents

Jobs in Education. 4

Main Office 8

Giving Guidance 12

Minding the Classroom 14

    Talking to a Teacher 16

Welcome to the Library 20

Supporting Roles at School 22

Inside the District Office. 26

At Work in School 29

    Extension: School Reporter! 30

    Glossary 31

    Index 32

Jobs in Education

The sidewalk in front of the school is filling with students. Some are yawning. Others are laughing. It is the start of another school day.

Schools are central to each community. In school, young people learn to read, write, and use math. Students explore history, science, and other countries. A school is an idea factory that produces new ways of thinking. From Alaska to Puerto Rico, the goals of schooling are the same. Teachers want to help students answer problems. Education is a **profession** in which teachers and others help students learn.

Learners for Life

Not only children go to school. Many adults sign up for classes in **community colleges** and **universities**. Grownups often want to develop work skills, such as how to use new **technology**. The need to learn does not end.

Opening the Doors

1600s New England colonies set up schools for boys. Parents pay **tuition** to send sons.

1700s Some towns open schools for girls.

1790 In Pennsylvania, new laws create free schooling for poor children.

1800s Massachusetts opens free schools and requires that all children attend.

1821 Boston Latin School, the first U.S. **public school** for older students, opens in Boston.

Learn By Doing

Most people learn best through activities and practice. Just thinking about ideas is not enough to fully understand meaning. So, teachers offer ways for students to try out concepts.

When planning lessons, teachers also look ahead. They wonder, "What will students need to get by and succeed in the future?" This is why many schools are adding in-depth science lessons. These are lessons in which students spend more time on each topic. People with science backgrounds are more likely to find jobs.

>> **You Know It!**

STEM stands for Science, Technology, Engineering, and Math. These studies are important for finding work in the 21st-century world.

School Work

Schooling is **mandatory** in this country and elsewhere. People aged 5 to 16 must attend classes in most U.S. states. However, some places start or end mandatory schooling at later ages.

Many successful people go to school for longer. They attend college for four years or more. They may earn advanced **degrees**.

How do we pay for schools?

People pay taxes to support public schools. Some parents choose to **homeschool** instead. Still others pay more money to send their children to **private schools**. A charter school is public, but it has different leaders than the others in an area. A magnet school has special classes.

Main Office

"Nobody notices what I do around here...
until I don't do it!"

Any visitor can see that a school is a busy place. Everyone has roles to play. Education has many levels and layers.

Generally, the main office is the business center in a school. The office workers answer phones. They order supplies and keep records. Almost anything you need to know about the school or students can be found in the main office.

"Every day is an adventure," says Maureen Selvaggio. She works in the office of a private school in New York state. "It's the children that make my job fun."

ADMINISTRATION

Taking Attendance

How many U.S. schools and students are there?

Public: **98,000**

Charter: **6,000**

Private: **31,000**

K–12 students: **50 million**

Cost of K–12 education: **$619 billion each year**

Source: U.S. Department of Education, 2014. All numbers approximated.

Friendly Faces

In small schools, one or two office workers complete many tasks. Sometimes, they help students who are sick. The workers call homes to check on student attendance.

The staff works to make sure parents, students, and other school workers get the right information. In many ways, the office workers are the "face" of the school. Visitors most often go to the main office first.

The Principal

Sometimes, the principal can be found in the office. More often, he or she is in the halls. He is checking classrooms or running meetings. She is training teachers or other workers.

One principal asked whether students could explain her work. A young child thought for a moment and then said the principal "talks on the speaker and picks up trash." In fact, principals are the leaders of schools.

> **"** Whenever I've [said that I taught English, the students] exclaim, 'You used to teach?'"
>
> —Illinois principal, in *Teaching Tolerance*

They set the rules. They keep records about students and school workers.

Path for a Principal

Want to help people do their best? Have ideas for how schools should run? Saying yes to these questions is the first step to becoming a principal.

Getting the Job

Skills

You'll need leadership, communication, and STEM skills (to read and report **data**, and to manage budgets).

Duties

Plan programs. Make rules. Follow education trends. Represent schools at meetings. Work with a budget and find funds for school activities.

Education

1. Need **bachelor's degree** and **license** or teaching certificate.
2. Work as classroom teacher.
3. To move up, you'll need a **master's degree**. Need license as an **administrator**.
4. May complete **doctoral degree**.

Giving Guidance

"Assessment and counseling allow me…to know a student and put together the various pieces of the bigger puzzle as to why the child is struggling in school."
—*from the blog of a California counselor*

In schools, counselors act as guides. They find help for troubled students. A school's counselors help students get along, succeed, and **excel**. These workers usually have their own offices, where they meet with students and families.

This work requires special **aptitudes**. Being a counselor is not easy. Over half of people who try the work quit in the first two years. It is important that counselors like communicating and helping people. They also should be able to read and understand data.

Career Counselors

Some counselors help older students plan which courses to take. Career counselors give special tests. The questions help students think about their likes and interests. A counselor can use the results of these tests to help a student plan courses for a future career.

What is the work like?

A counselor's day may start with an early meeting with a parent. The worker may report to the principal afterward.

The counselor may then fill out reports. There may be time for a quick lunch. Then, he or she will observe students in a classroom.

STEM studies are important for this job. Counselors need to know human sciences. They need math skills for reading and reporting test results.

Minding the Classroom

"My favorite part of teaching is having the opportunity to show students how important they are."
—Scott Parker, teacher in Hill City, Kansas

Teachers, who work in classrooms, are at the heart of the school. In elementary schools, each teacher covers many subjects. He or she may teach math in the morning and social studies in the afternoon.

In middle and high school, students go from class to class. Each teacher covers certain subjects. You may have one teacher for science and another for history. The instructors see many students daily.

You Know It!

The White House is calling for 100,000 math and science teachers in the next decade.

Subject Matters

Teachers give lectures and lead activities. They help students in computer labs. Teachers show different ways to process and use information.

After class, a teacher may meet with students and families to discuss learning **strategies**. He or she may review papers and grade tests. Teachers also search for new ideas to use in the classroom.

Why do some teachers coach?

Coaching can be a way to earn extra money. But coaching also is a chance to see students from another perspective.

One group asked teachers why they coach. Their number-one reason: *Through coaching I get a sense of satisfaction in teaching and watching young people grow and develop.*

Talking to a Teacher

Scott Parker of Graham County, Kansas, teaches technology in both elementary school and junior high. Technology, he says, can be defined as "applied science."

1. What do you want students to learn?

Technology is really a tool. It is very important for me to teach students how to use this tool. Learning technology means students are gaining skills they can use in any area of their lives.

Technology is always changing. So, I think that teaching **problem-solving skills** is important. That way, students can adapt to whatever is new.

It is very possible that a student I have now may one day have a career that hasn't even been invented yet!

2. What is your day like?

My teaching day is different from many other teachers. Not only do I teach classes, but I also help teachers with their computer needs when I can. I coordinate much of what teachers and others do with all the computers in our schools.

Sometimes, I'll be teaching class. Then, I may find myself needing to troubleshoot a technology issue in another building, right after my class is finished.

3 ## What is the best part?

It is an honor to be in a job where I can show students how good life is. The future is always there, with an endless list of possibilities.

It is like school is not just the building that students attend. It's now the whole world they live in, and beyond. It's just ready to be explored!

Teaching Assistants

Some teachers have assistants. These aides help keep order, which can be a big help in big classes. The assistants also give extra help as needed. For example, some students cannot see or hear well. An aide may help them use special tools to understand the lessons.

Most students struggle with lessons at one time. So, some schools also offer **tutors**. This kind of worker reviews schoolwork with students. The extra attention from a tutor can help the students succeed.

>> You Know It!

The student population is expected to grow. One way that schools will deal with this is by hiring more assistants.

Tech Touch

Assistants often keep track of how well students perform. So, it helps to have technology skills. The tools classroom aides use include the following:

- Computers
- Training software
- Data software
- Spreadsheets
- Tools for students with special challenges

What is blended learning?

Today, there is a great deal of talk about blended learning. This is a mix of face-to-face learning and online learning. More schools are providing lessons on computer networks. Teaching aides are stepping in to help students who get their lessons online.

Welcome to the Library

"You have to like to teach to be a happy school librarian."
—Barb Powers, Arlington Heights, Illinois, librarian

The school's library is a large, open classroom. Library workers help people find books and other tools. They show students how to use the internet safely.

"You can create a place where learning is fun. It's the one place in school where kids get to choose," says Barb Powers. She enjoys her library job.

In studies of education, school libraries or media centers have been tied to student performance. Schools with **media specialists** tend to show better on test results. Their students have better research skills and perform better on tests.

Contents of the Work

A librarian's role has three parts, says Powers. One is teaching. Another is to be a manager. This includes collecting books and creating special reading programs. The third part is helping to come up with what will be taught in the classrooms. A key role is testing new models for teaching.

"The librarian can help the teacher come up with ideas for using technology," says Powers.

Score!

Michigan elementary students with higher test scores were **4 times** as likely to visit the library.

New Mexico middle schools with higher scores were **2 times** as likely to offer network access to libraries from classrooms and home.

Supporting Roles at School

"You can't scare me. I drive a school bus."

Many kinds of workers support the schools, helping students and other workers. For example, bus drivers take students to and from school and events. Without drivers and other workers, schools could not stay open and students would not be safe.

Guards

Guards often need special training and licenses. They keep track of people who enter the school grounds. The guards make rounds to keep students and workers safe. Guards also play a role in emergencies, such as storms or fires. They help keep things under control.

Nurses

Nurses set up health programs, teach health and wellness classes, and reach out to the community with school health information. They make wellness plans for students with ongoing health problems. For example, nurses set times for students to take medicines.

Maintenance Workers

The people in maintenance take care of both buildings and machines. For example, they may fix pipes that break. Sometimes, the work includes taking care of the lawns and parking lots. Without these workers, the school buildings would fall apart.

Custodians

These workers do the cleaning and are in charge of upkeep. They also go into action at school events, such as setting up chairs and tables. Without these workers, garbage would line the hallways. The custodians help keep schools clean and healthy.

There and Back

Transportation workers are in charge of safe travels for students and school workers. A **rural** school may have just one driver, but large schools need many transportation workers. For example, someone may be placed in charge of fixing broken buses.

Bus drivers need special training. This especially matters when roads are crowded or wet. Some drivers navigate roads filled with traffic. A large bus does not move as easily as a car. Drivers also need to know how to do basic engine checks. They must be able to watch kids, too. The large mirrors that drivers use help them see what is happening inside, as well as outside, the bus.

On the Menu

In schools, food service workers play important roles. To be healthy, young people need fresh and healthful foods. Eating well has been tied to better schoolwork.

The cafeteria must be run as a business. The workers need to be able to feed the students and adults in the school for a set amount of money each week. In fact, many schools hire companies for this work. They need experts in food service.

Who plans the meals?

A nutritionist or a dietician plans the meals. These workers have taken many science classes. They know why eating right helps human bodies. In addition, these workers understand business. Nutritionists and dieticians need STEM skills to plan healthy balanced meals on a budget.

Inside the District Office

New York City has its own schools with more than one million students. The city schools cost more than $20 million to operate each year. However, most of the country is not part of a big city. So, the land is divided into parts called districts. Each district holds power over its schools.

Some educators serve as administrators, or managers, in district offices. One leader may serve the district as the **supervisor**. Yet, many other people report to him or her. Each one leads some aspect of the schools, such as sports or elementary school subjects.

» You Know It!

Largest U.S. School District
New York City Department of Education

Second Largest
Los Angeles Unified School District

Third Largest
Chicago Public Schools

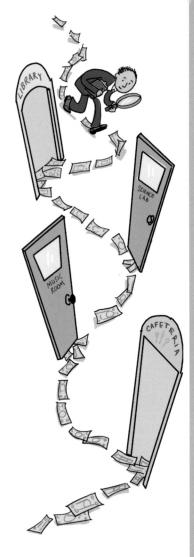

Take a Position

Many schools have a director of operations. This person tries to make sure the workers do well. He or she also makes decisions about the things purchased for the schools. For example, the director may study how many and what type of computers are needed in each school.

Another school leader may be in charge of the **curriculum** in elementary schools. Someone else may lead the middle school teachers. Schools have many career needs.

What do accountants do?

School accountants make audits. Those are studies of how money came in and went out.

Community Input

School boards or similar groups help run schools. Members of the community join the boards or they may be elected to school boards. Most schools have parent groups as well. For example, a parent group may raise money to fix a playground or buy musical instruments.

All Business

Jill Cohn is the business manager of a group of preschools in Northern California. Like many school workers, she has many roles. "I wear many hats each day," she says.

She needs both math skills and people skills to do her work. Cohn studies the size of each class. She tries to balance the number of boys and girls. She considers the ages of the children as well to create a balance.

At Work in School

Business Manager. Head of Operations. Principal. Special Needs Teacher. Teaching Assistant. Tech Teacher. Librarian.

The titles are different from one place to another. But the hopes are the same. Students hope to get an education. School leaders hope to find people who can help their students.

Are you interested in helping people?

Do you like to go to school?

Can you see yourself in college learning to do the work needed in a school?

Perhaps you will one day work on the job . . . in a school.

Extension
School Reporter!

Think about the workers in your school. Is there someone in a job you would like to understand better? Ask for a time to meet the person.

Before

Consider things you would like to know more about. Look in books and safe online sources for background information.

Write five or six questions. Test each one. Make sure it cannot be answered with just a yes or no. Use questions that will give you interesting answers.

During

Be on time. Bring paper and a writing tool. If possible, record the conversation. Ask your questions politely. Listen carefully. Take notes. Say "thank you" when done.

After

Look over your materials. Think about details you noticed. For example, if the phone rang, take note. Writing about the ringing phone could help demonstrate that the job is busy.

Write an introduction. Make sure to cover basic facts: *who, what, where, when,* and *why*. Then, share your questions and their answers with your class and family.

Glossary

administration: process of running an organization; those who do this work

aptitudes: abilities or talents

bachelor's degree: earned for three to five years of study after high school

community colleges: places of education which tend to offer degrees for two years of study after high school

curriculum: courses students take

data: facts and figures

degrees: notices awarded to people for advanced study

doctoral degree: earned for highest level of study, showing ability to teach at the university level

engineering: science concerned with building or using machines and structures

excel: to do better than others

homeschool: to teach at home

license: notice of permission to perform something

mandatory: required by law

master's degree: earned for mastery of subject at least one year beyond bachelor's degree

media specialists: librarians who teach research methods

private schools: places of education not run by government officials and not paid for with public tax money

problem-solving skills: using methods in an orderly way to get results

profession: work that involves serving or helping others

public schools: places of education supported by tax money and run by government officials

rural: outside towns or cities

strategies: plans of action

supervisor: person in charge of school, government, or business operations

technology: science applied to life and industry

tuition: fee charged for schooling

tutors: people who give lessons in private

universities: places of higher learning which provide advanced degrees

Index

accountant 27

administrator 26

blended learning 19

Boston English 5

bus driver 24

charter school 7

coaching 15

Cohn, Jill 28

community college 5

counselor 12, 13

custodian 23

dietician 25

guard 22

homeschool 7

librarian 20, 29

magnet school 7

media specialist 21

nurse 22

Parker, Scott 16, 17

Powers, Barb 20, 21

principal 10, 11, 29

STEM 6, 11, 13, 25

teacher 14, 15

teaching assistant . . 18, 29

technology 16

university 5

>> Meet the Author

Jessica Cohn has made a career of writing and editing materials for young people, covering varied topics, from social studies and science to poetry. If you ask her, Cohn will tell you that she feels lucky to be on the job in educational publishing. Each day, she discovers something new to learn and someone with an interesting story—and then gets to share the information. Jessica and her family reside in California. When not working, she enjoys hiking, helping her local library, and exploring the country.